Love & a Loaded Gun

Love & a Loaded Gun

Poems by
Emily Rose Cole

Minerva Rising • Atlanta
2017

Published by
Minerva Rising Press
9501 Bessie Coleman Blvd
#21082
Tampa, FL 33622-1082

ISBN: 978-0-9990254-2-0

www.minervarising.com

Dedication

For Leda & Persephone, for Joan of Arc & Judy Garland, for Princess Peach & Lois Lane & every other woman who's ever been made to keep her mouth shut.

Contents

Foreword

Each winner over the course of Minerva Rising's Poetry Chapbook contest has picked up the mantle of our "Dare to Be" theme and veritably marched through the streets. From Victorian women in love, to the parlor tricks of a revolutionary queen and the survival song of a mother fighting to wrest her child from certain abuse, our press has not shied away from courageous heroines telling their stories in their own voices. Our latest book in the series rises to the occasion, with its page after page of persona poems that smoke like cooling jets, each one an ember smoldering with complex characters who will bite your head off, then stroke your trembling hands. 2017 winning poet Emily Rose Cole has written of women—Dorothy, Demeter, Persephone, Judy, Bonnie, Guinevere, and more—women you know but now will see in a whole new light, women who are just as fierce as they are vulnerable. Their temerity is tempered with a side of hesitation that simmers below the surface. You want to invite them over for coffee but know they won't sit still long enough for the steam to clear. Once it does, you may recognize yourself in the mirror you hold up on every page.

> When I was three, my mother caught a bluebird
> and stitched her into my throat while I slept

And so begins *Love & a Loaded Gun*, Cole's "own precious, blue voice" and Minerva Rising's latest and most captivating "Dare to Be" chapbook winner yet. But the voice is less precious than piercing, less blue than bold. Like a ride on a literary tilt-a-whirl, these poems take you upside down and inside the minds of some of our greatest and most notable fictional, historical, and mythical *femmes fatales* gone even invites you to make love to Joan of Arc, a girl who "could bathe all of France in the holy milk of her eyes." Reader, I dare you to read that poem and not taste cream on your tongue.

These poems are about characters from history, pop culture,

mythology, and the literary canon who are exploding for one reason or another—either because love is so impossible, because they are driven by rage to commit acts of revenge, or because they feel the burden of being a woman whose role it is to bear the world. They are also connected by apron strings, by bird feathers, by prayer, by love and its antidote, the loaded gun we point at our own weaknesses as well as our social preconceptions about feminism and womanhood. This collection, guised as myriad voices through time, serves as megaphone for the ages. This book has "arrived armed with love / & a loaded gun." Our winning poet takes aim with the weapon of her words, "a bullet they won't ever see coming," and shoots a hole straight through the ceiling of glass.

Emily Shearer
Minerva Rising Poetry Editor
July 2017

Judy Garland Speaks of Her Early Career

When I was three, my mother caught a bluebird
and stitched her into my throat while I slept, seam

of sinew sewn to wing. Blood pooled into my pillow.
I woke with feathers shot through the sticky ropes of my hair.

At first, I had trouble swallowing, but I learned to gulp
around the beating-hearted bulge beneath my chin.

When she sang, I turned mockingbird, mimicking
her muffled trills, the blue croon of her warbling.

At thirteen, I took off: landed job after job, chased
Benzedrine with Hershey kisses. On nights blurred

salty by vodka and sleeping pills, we'd hum lullabies
in A-minor and I'd finger the scars threaded to my neck,

the ones that held her inside me. At sixteen, I crammed my toes
into a pair of spangled silver heels, threw the deadbolt

across my trailer door. I pried those careful stiches out
with a rust-edged steak knife, and stained my shoes red

as she surged from my throat, wings oiled in blood,

song bright as polished tin. She was gone

when they found me, escaped through a back window.
She left me with a throat full of feathers

and my own precious, blue voice.

Leda Leaves Manhattan

Three days after it happened, I grab a greyhound
going west. All I have: a duffel stuffed with socks, t-shirts,
oil paints, a coffee-stained photo of my mother. A little cash.

I spark Marlboro menthols in the lavatory, spit smoke
into the no-flush toilet. Stench curls and thickens.
Fluorescents buzz overhead. The floor lurches beneath

my feet. Nothing is steady anymore. The door clicks shut;
I slump back to my window seat. I need to be landlocked,
waterless. I have friends in Kansas City. I'll crash

on couches, find some doctor to take care of me,
if it comes to that. I'll pursue a new hobby: take a shotgun
to the edge of a lake and shoot at every shadow of wings.

Rapunzel Learns to Build

i.

My mother built her tower out of baby teeth
broken on stale communion wafers, out of dogs
choked by chicken bones, empty medicine cabinets,
every lullaby her mother never sang her.

When she got me, she mixed a mortar of bent
needles, busted harp strings, and porcupine
quills pulled from beneath her fingernails.

One day, she told me, *gold dust will pool in the hollow
of your tongue. Roses will track their roots in your spine.
Your body will chip like shale rock chiseled by rain.*

ii.

She shut me in. No door. One locked window.
A keyhole cut in the shape of my name.

I stayed inside for years, afraid of anything
that carried its shadow too close to itself.
My mother hoisted baskets of mint and dill.

She wrote notes that ended with *for your own good*
and planted morning glories that opened like eyes.

iii.

When a prince arrived, he used words like *trapped*
and *escape*. I offered a rope woven from daisy stems,
but he said my hair was stronger.

The shorn end of the braid thumped the grass
like a feathered body striking stones. Years later,
after he left me, I carved a hole in my tongue.

I came home. The tower had fallen. My mother's last gift:
a handful of pebbles shaping a word: *grow*.
I built my tower out of nettles and closed doors
and dropped seeds into my eyes.

iv.

Now, red petals curl behind my teeth.
Pollen smears my lips and bees
drone at the corners of my mouth.

I swallow secrets that harden into keys.
All night, I listen to locks sliding shut.

Red Molly Claims Her Prize

Says James, in my opinion, there's nothing in this world
Beats a '52 Vincent and a red headed girl.
–Richard Thompson, "1952 Vincent Black Lightning"

I was his junkyard queen crowned in rust & leather,
our lady of peeling paint & busted engines. The first time
he took me out, his Vincent hummed through my thighs
like a sickness & it was all I wanted.

I'm a dangerous man, he said, & I told him I fell in love
with his knife wounds, each shiner & split lip I'd dress
in alcohol. He knocked back fistfuls of fennel
seeds swollen with Jameson, said they were good for breath
& courage, as if he needed more of either.

I let him open my ear with his teeth,
fill my hollows with his scent, menthols & gasoline.
I'm a smart girl. I knew what road we growled over.

Two days before his 22nd birthday, my second cousin's
shotgun peeled his lungs apart like a knife slitting peach flesh
from pit. At the hospital, he dangled the key on his ring
finger, smeared it red as his sheets: *I got no further use
for these.* I did my duty, salted his chest with tears.

Coffin barely closed, I swung onto his prized machine &
rode my inheritance hard, tasted wind stuck to the roof
of my mouth, savored the power of drive.

Pharaoh's Wife Mourns Her Son

"There shall be a great cry throughout all Egypt..."
—Exodus 11.6

I anoint his body with dust
and locust wings.

The Nile spits grief
like an open vein.

Maggots writhe
in the walls, in the bread,
in the ears of cats.

Leaves gape like empty mouths—
no fruit on the vine. No pearls
of grain in the storehouse.

Mothers stack their children like cords of ash
and cedar. We drop their cinders down
our throats, as if returning our sons
to our bodies could make us birth them again.

Husband, hook open your eyes.
See where your crooked hand has led us.

Demeter, On Spring

Everything is about loss. The bees, too long overwintered,
still beat their wings double-time to preserve their queen.
I would take them

as I've taken everything else—the hawk's eyes eaten,
the farmer's toenails curled in death, his wife's greasy lip-
print on his whiskey glass—except you always loved bees
& I wanted you not to have them.

I am kind. I don't keep the lake from rifting.
Beneath the weakening ice, a flounder's scales
are yellowing back to life. Soon you, too,
will unfreeze. Yes, daughter. I do want you

back. My laudanum. My satellite. Buried seed
pearl, mine. But can't I love this deprivation
a little longer? There is joy

in taking. Even from you.

Poem in Which You Are Joan of Arc's Lover

You expect it to begin like a battle,
but there's no bite in her. She doesn't kiss
you, doesn't coo like the girl she is.

You jut your hips like you own her.
It's strange to you that her tunic smells
of myrrh and smoke and saltpeter.

When you try to frame her face
in your fingers, she pins you
with her eyes until you do as you're told:

plus dur, plus fort, plus, plus, plus.
You almost expect her to cry
out, but when she unhooks

her mouth and flashes her eyes,
blank and white as salt, she does not name
saints or gods, but fortresses—

Saint Loup, Jean-le-Blanc—and tactics
gasped in a strange language: *Advance
advance. Hold the line. Steady now. Steady.*

She makes you feel as if you're all

the army she needs, until her vision
clears and she's not a vessel anymore,

just a girl waving you to the door,
scrambling to scrawl heaven's help
on the map tucked under her pillow.

You know now that if you sink
your hands into her hair,
God will tongue lightning

down your back, that only a girl
like her could bathe all of France
in the holy milk of her eyes.

Bonnie remembers the first time

That night, you smelled like the crook
of a dead man's neck, like the breath of cologne
he spritzed there before he kissed his wife goodbye.

He couldn't have known a piece of his lung would smooch
the sidewalk later that day. You nudged me awake
with the butt of your Colt, grin cocked

& loaded, said, *Baby, we gotta skip town.* I heard
the rattlesnake in your chest shimmy & whisper
in my mama's voice, *girl, you better run.*

Our fingers locked & poised like hammers in a gun.
Clyde, when you ordered me that first whiskey
sour, I knew we would die with lead in our mouths.

Clarice Starling Proves Her Love
(A Recipe for Ortolan Bunting)

I.

Swell of wings in nets.

She is red-mouthed & yellow-headed.
Sparrow-sized, the same length
as your lover's clenched fist.

Stop your ears against her frightened trilling:
You must forget that she is capable of song. Nestle her

in your palms. Feel her fresh heart gunning
through the slats of her thread-thin ribs.

II.

Fill a trough with soft figs, oats, & millet.
When your lover says, *Be brave, Clarice,*
pretend that this qualifies as an act of bravery.
Hold her down. Pinch her beak. Pluck out

her eyes with a needle
        or a pair of narrow-nosed pliers.

Let him lick the blood from the crest

of your thumb. Try to smile.

III.

Blindness will unlock in her a fierce hunger.
Refresh her feed eight times a day. Don't linger

near the cage to watch her gorge. Don't think
of the bars, of their frantic rattle when she rams
her head down into the trough. Of how thin
you thought they were. Leave the room.

Double lock the door behind you.

IV.

Fill a deep snifter with Armagnac.
Do not drink any. It is not yours.

> None of this is yours.

Retrieve her. Perhaps her head will roll
languid, like your lover's does
when he's just waking.

Plunge her in headfirst. Fill her lungs.
If you must,

> imagine baptism.

V.

Settle her in a shallow dish. Stoke your oven.
Watch the flames smelt her feathers to a sheen.

Roast for exactly eight minutes at 350 degrees.

VI.

Snap the napkin open. Crease a cowl
over your head. He'll tell you it'll capture
the incense of her juices. He won't tell you
it'll hide your gluttony from God. But you'll know.

Cradle her in your jaw, like a snake ready to swallow
a kill. Close your eyes, but don't pray yet.
Clamp your teeth around the beak & bite it off clean.
Treat its clatter like the first notes of a symphony.

Enjoy this, the rending of her exquisite flesh,
veins shuddering across your teeth,
each needle of bone coppering your gums
with blood. Obey when he tells you
to save the lungs for last.

> When you gash them open, brandy sweet as song
> spilling down your throat, pray two prayers at once:
> *O Lord, thank You & O Lord, forgive me.*

VII.

Let him kiss you in the dark.
Run your tongue along the lacerations
she pricked open.

Taste him.

Taste her.

Know that you are both responsible.

Dorothy Gale, After the Funeral

These days, my bones are thrush-thin & all I want
is a winnowing. I want skin loosening at the small
of my back, wind lifting me like an exaltation

of ragweed. What a blessing, to be carried
like a child in a womb. Aunt Em fell asleep

in the earth & now I'm as still as a beating heart.
I sleep in a bedroll that swaddles me like batwings
& I keep the radio tuned to the weather.

The huckleberries that sugar my tongue burn
in my blue mouth. No place feels like home.

Now, another storm kicks its heels
in my face—gunmetal clouds close
into thunderheads, pines hurl down
their sap-ripe ribs. I enter the field,
rain lashing my eyelids shut,

scarecrow my arms, palms out,
& speak to the storm like a mare
I used to ride when I was young.

I tell it, *I don't want to be here.*
I tell it, *We are the same kind of runaway.*

I tell it, *Take me back.*

The Snow Queen Takes a Hostage

i. *what his grandmother said*

Winter distorts everything. Swarms of snow-bees shake
their wings, coat each girder and shingle in slick down.

Watch for the Snow Queen, darling boy, but keep your distance.
She can prick your chest with a sickle and fill your throat
with ice. If she finds you, think of climbing trees barefoot,
think of sunlight kissing the cups of daffodils,
clean sheets, bubbling kettles, candles guttering at dusk.

ii. *the Snow Queen arrives*

She steals into town like a magician: all misdirection,
and fills the sky with falling mirrors. Daughter of the north
wind and arctic sea, her bones are packed with the corpses
of leaves, teeth brighter than fern frost.
Her eyes pass over a locked window.

iii. *what she offers him*

One kiss, and I'll flash
freeze memory at the roots, erase
every name your mother called you,
every bottle warmed by your father's lips.

Leave this place where rats skitter
through your walls and moths tongue holes
in your favorite coat. Ride with me.

I promise ice-blossoms on every window,
new skates sharp as a snowflake's edge,
a palace where nothing shatters, nothing
molders, nothing ever melts.

Come closer, child.

Guinevere, Burning

I take him in my hand and imagine myself
a sculptor—wheel, clay, distant rustle
of fire. An act of will, this shaping. My will

more than his. I know he loves me everywhere
but here, bedshades half-drawn, a scythe
of moonlight carving up his thigh.

Three years we've been without
consummation—my skin: iron, his: rust.
No tincture or spell. No ritual but practice

and defeat. No heir until I'm queen enough
to warrant conquering. Lips, breath. My tongue
a lathe. At court, women murmur of ruin—

breached stockings, wrecked petticoats,
a militia of bruises moiling beneath their slips.
What must it be like to be desired

 to the point of violence? Under me,
Arthur gives up, rolls over. No kiss.
Sheets tight, my hands fashion their own

pleasure, a vase with a crumpled mouth,

turning, turning. His is not the name I shape
my lips around as I come and come and come.

The Target Girl Learns to Eat Knives

From the center of the wheel
that creaks like a bedspring,
you watch the knife leave his hand,
whorl in spirals tight as spandex.
His near-misses pin your hair,
notch the arch of your neck, grooved
teeth shuddering against your cheeks.
The wheel moans like the woman
you found contorted in his sheets.
You let your breath rise like a lion
tamer's wrist before the lash. You know
where he's aiming.
You open your mouth—

Daily Planet Exclusive

for Superman

Believe me when I say that he lies
like a crumpled lily in my arms each night,
that when I press my chest to him I feel the bullet
of his heart speeding through his back.

Believe me when I say he is afraid.

Sometimes, when he thinks I'm sleeping,
he rustles the sheets and vanishes to the other
side of the world, just so he can be sure
that the sun has risen somewhere,
its chip of molten gold still close
enough for him to touch, if he wanted to.

Believe me that he's too conscious of what strength,
that sheer curtain of steel, cannot save:

those men who jump from highrises
and bridges when he's across town,

those women who lash themselves
to the tracks two minutes before the train
hurtles in, daring him with their cries: *Save me,*

I am holding you responsible.

and me—the strange spots on my brain
scan, the red milk running in my spine—
a kind of falling from which there is no rescue.

Believe me when I say he carries guilt like a moon
of Jupiter hanging from his neck, that some nights,

when I trace the double bend of the letter
branded above his heart and lower my teeth

to hiss his name, his thumbs light
into my palms, and he pleads *No,*
Lois, call me anything but that.

The Contortionist

Tonight, I visit the bigtop alone,
the black air thick with lightning

and fryer oil. I take center ring,
lie flat under the trapeze rig
and pinwheel an elbow

beneath a leg, tip my chin to kiss
the sag of the net, and look
for the boy

            who jumped last year,

                      a freak

accident, they said. Except

I saw the whipped tiger's eyes
in his eyes, saw him cupping
the strongman's cock

            like he meant it.

He told me once that he only felt alive
in the air, spare body hung
between bar   and bar.

        I called him Anya,

like he asked, but I didn't think of him

    as *she* until she was sprawled
    on the loose dirt, arm pinned
    beneath a knee like the spent
    arch of a ballerina's foot.

But when they switched
her eyelids shut and said   *he's gone,*
I didn't dare correct them.

Now, she trembles
   at the platform's edge
      like a shadow. Under the net,
          I pleat my feet like palms in prayer

and I wonder if she can still smell

    popcorn and wet elephant shit,
    if she still loves the calliope
    and the way a tongue collapses
    cotton candy, its fragile net
              of melting sugar.

Anya lifts her heels,
        poised to leap.

I see her

        suspended,   blurred

fingers opening

      for a bar

           that will not   swing

Persephone Returns

This before everything: shame.
I disappeared, so she fettered the earth

with snow. She tried to drag Hell
to her doorstep: everything dead—
cattle fallen in the frost-wrecked fields,
the choked river's familiar moan,
icicles spearing the trees. What did I expect?

To leave a hemorrhage
of violets wherever I walked?

No. A lost son is called *prodigal.*
A lost daughter is just called *lost.*

This is how she greets me:
shoulder jutted to the doorjamb,
fists bolted to her hips.

Here I am: a daughter: loved
& rejected all at once.

Your Princess Leaves the Castle

Trust me, honey, I know this hellhole better
than you do. I've spent half my life locked
under a turtle shell. While you bounced
in the back way through the pipes, I opened
doors with my hairpins and explored. I know
this place. And I'm sick of it.

For years you've solved every problem
by stepping on it. It's simple for you: pulverize
the henchmen, emasculate the boss, watch me
swoon. Well, joke's on you, Mario. I quit.

While you were doing mushrooms and grubbing
coins, I learned to hotwire an engine in under
a minute. You'd barely recognize me dressed in blue
jeans and flannel, hair bobbed. I don't pretend
I'm safe—the road I'm clipping over is littered
banana peels and walking bombs.

But I can tell you this: I'm not
in another castle. Don't come looking.

Black Widow Explains

Love is for children.
–Natasha Romanoff, *The Avengers*

As a child I learned that what makes me a girl
makes me a threat. I copied the saw-toothed smiles
of kitchen knives & juiced lemons to lighten my hair.

I learned how not to bleed & when
to cant my head like a kitten.

Does it matter, what made me?

    Permafrost gripped the taiga
    when he took me, spruce & larches
    thatched in ice. *Nyet, nyet,*
    he wheezed as I reached
    for a *pyrizhky.* His voice: a rumble
    of wheels & smoke. My heart:
    a drowning rat.

Everything is a disguise—black dress slit
to my thigh, lips bright as the cherry
stem laced on my tongue. Not a person,
not to a certain kind of man. Just a woman.

When I say *I escaped*, I mean
I killed him. I will not tell you how.

It's not hard to be a spy. All women are made of muscle
& trauma. We know how to doe our eyes & shut
the fuck up so a man won't kill us.

I give them just what they expect—*dumb bitch*
easy bitch, dirty bitch—let them boil me down
to a curvy silhouette. They never suspect

that I arrived armed with love
& a loaded gun, wearing clichés
like Chanel to blind them to the bullet
they won't ever see coming.

Acknowledgments

Many thanks to the editors of the following publications where some of these poems have appeared or will appear, sometimes in slightly different versions or under different titles:

Bluestem — "Daily Planet Exclusive"

FreezeRay — "Your Princess Leaves the Castle"

Gingerbread House — "Clarice Starling Proves Her Love (A Recipe for Ortolan Bunting)" (As: "What to Do When He Asks You to Prove Your Love (A Recipe for Ortolan Bunting)")

IthacaLit — "Dorothy Gale, After the Funeral" (As: "Self-Portrait as Dorothy Gale")

Jabberwock Review — "Judy Garland Speaks of Her Early Career" (Winner, 2014 Nancy D. Hargrove Editor's Prize)

Neon — "Red Molly Claims Her Prize" & "The Snow Queen Takes a Hostage"

Nimrod — "Poem in Which You Are Joan of Arc's Lover" & "The Contortionist" (Finalists, 2015 Pablo Neruda Prize)

NonBinary Review — "Black Widow Explains"

Passages North — "Bonnie remembers the first time" (As: "She remembers the first time")

The Pinch — "Persephone Returns" "(As: Self-Portrait as Persephone Returning")

Philadelphia Stories — "Rapunzel Learns to Build" (Winner, 2014 Sandy Crimmins Award, As: "Self-Portrait as Rapunzel")

Ruminate — "Pharaoh's Wife Mourns Her Son"

SOFTBLOW — "The Target Girl Learns to Eat Knives"

Word Riot — "Leda Leaves Manhattan"

Many thanks to the patient and dedicated staff at Minerva Rising, and the following individuals, whose careful eyes and generous hearts helped shape these poems: Brenda Johnson, M. Brett Gaffney, Avery Guess, Seanse Ducken, Ruth Awad, Jonathan Travelstead, Laura Rufno, Lucien Darjeun Meadows, Robert Parrott, Teresa Dzieglewicz, Jacquelyn Zeng, Anna Knowles, Jacqueline Zhang, Kirk Schuleter, Alyssha Nelson, Meghann Plunkett, Mary Kate Varnau, John McCarthy, Andrew Hemmert, Chelsey Harris, David Fairbanks, Cole Bucciaglia, Jessica Suchon, Josh Myers, Lathan Ehlers, Andy Harper, Josh Bontrager, Austin Kodra, Phil Martin, James Dunlap, Andy Leeming, Kelson Hatfeld, and especially Toni Judnitch, the world's most extraordinary roommate.

Particular thanks to Judy Jordan, Allison Joseph, Jon Tribble, and Jennifer Key, my wonderful teachers at Southern Illinois University Carbondale, and to Rochelle Hurt, without whom I would never have become so fascinated in persona poems in the first place.

Finally, thanks to my dad, Clifford Cole, and my stepmom, Pamela West, who have been endlessly supportive of my work, even when it contains a high amount of violence and dead birds.

Author Biography

Emily Rose Cole holds an MFA from Southern Illinois University Carbondale. Her poems have appeared in *The Pinch, Nimrod, Southern Indiana Review,* and *Spoon River Poetry Review,* among others. She teaches composition, creative writing, and pedagogy at the University of Cincinnati, where she is completing a doctorate in poetry and disability studies.